Ready for Math

Ready for
Fractions
and Decimals

Rebecca Wingard-Nelson

FREE WORKSHEETS AVAILABLE AT www.enslow.com

Enslow Elementary
an imprint of
Enslow Publishers, Inc.
40 Industrial Road
Box 398
Berkeley Heights, NJ 07922
USA

http://www.enslow.com

Enslow Elementary, an imprint of Enslow Publishers, Inc.

Enslow Elementary® is a registered trademark of Enslow Publishers, Inc.

Original edition published as *Fractions and Decimals Made Easy* in 2005.

Library of Congress Cataloging-in-Publication Data

Wingard-Nelson, Rebecca.
   [Fractions and decimals made easy]
   Ready for fractions and decimals / Rebecca Wingard-Nelson; [illustrations: Tom LaBaff].
     p. cm. — (Ready for math)
   Originally published under the title Fractions and decimals made easy; Berkeley Heights, NJ : Enslow Elementary, c2005.
   Summary: "Learn the basic fundamentals of adding, subtracting, multiplying and dividing using fractions and decimals"—Provided by publisher.
   Includes bibliographical references and index.
   ISBN 978-0-7660-4247-6
   1. Fractions—Juvenile literature. 2. Decimal fractions—Juvenile literature. I. LaBaff, Tom, ill. II. Title.
   QA117.W56 2014
   513.2'6—dc23

                                2012038739

Future editions:
Paperback ISBN: 978-1-4644-0437-5
Single-User PDF ISBN: 978-1-4646-1238-1

EPUB ISBN: 978-1-4645-1238-4
Multi-User PDF ISBN: 978-0-7660-5870-5

Printed in the United States of America

102013 Lake Book Manufacturing, Inc., Melrose Park, IL

10 9 8 7 6 5 4 3 2 1

To Our Readers: We have done our best to make sure all Internet addresses in this book were active and appropriate when we went to press. However, the author and the publisher have no control over and assume no liability for the material available on those Internet sites or on other Web sites they may link to. Any comments or suggestions can be sent by e-mail to comments@enslow.com or to the address on the back cover.

♻ Enslow Publishers, Inc., is committed to printing our books on recycled paper. The paper in every book contains 10% to 30% post-consumer waste (PCW). The cover board on the outside of each book contains 100% PCW. Our goal is to do our part to help young people and the environment too!

Illustration Credits: Tom LaBaff
Cover Illustration: Tom LaBaff

Contents

Introduction

Math is all around, and an important part of anyone's life. You use math when you are playing games, cooking food, spending money, telling time, reading music, or doing any other activity that uses numbers. Even finding a television channel uses math!

Fractions and Decimals Are Everywhere

You use fractions every day. Every time you use the word *half*, you are talking about a fraction! Measurements often use fractions. For example, a pencil could be $6\frac{3}{4}$ inches long; you might need $\frac{1}{2}$ cup of sugar for cookies; and your dog might weigh $21\frac{1}{3}$ pounds.

Decimals are an important part of our money system. Money amounts in dollars and cents are written as decimals. Sports statistics, such as batting averages and race times, are also given as decimal numbers. The metric system is a way to measure using decimals, instead of fractions.

Using This Book

This book can be used to learn or review fractions and decimals at your own speed. It can be used on your own or with a friend, tutor, or parent. Get ready to discover math . . . made easy!

What Is a Fraction?

Fractions are numbers that stand for part of a whole. A fraction may show part of one whole thing.

This chocolate cake was cut into 6 equal pieces.

One piece of the cake is gone.

You can use a fraction to show how much of the cake is gone.

$\dfrac{1}{6}$ piece of cake is gone
pieces of cake in the whole cake

$\dfrac{1}{6}$ of the cake is gone.

A fraction may show part of one whole group.

This is one whole group of elephants. Some of the elephants are pink. You can use a fraction to show how many in the group of elephants are pink.

$\dfrac{3}{8}$ elephants are pink
     elephants are in the group

$\dfrac{3}{8}$ of the elephants are pink.

Fraction Terms

All fractions are made of two numbers, a top number and a bottom number.

The bottom number is the denominator. It tells how many equal parts are in the whole. The top number is the numerator. It tells how many parts you are talking about.

To help you remember which is which, think, "*D* is for *downstairs* and *denominator*, so the denominator goes on the bottom."

numerator ⟶ $\dfrac{\mathbf{1}}{\mathbf{4}}$ ⟵ number of parts of you are talking about
denominator ⟶ ⟵ number of equal parts in the whole

When you read a fraction, read the top number first. Then read the bottom number using words like *half, thirds, fourths,* or *fifths.*

$$\frac{1}{4}$$

This fraction is read as one fourth.

$\frac{2}{3}$ of this pie is left.

The fraction $\frac{2}{3}$ is read as two thirds.

The bottom number, 3, tells you there are three equal pieces in the whole pie. The top number, 2, tells you that two of the parts are left.

$\frac{1}{2}$ of these socks are dirty.

The fraction $\frac{1}{2}$ is read as one half.

The bottom number, 2, tells you there are two socks in the whole group. The top number, 1, tells you that one of the socks is dirty.

Proper Fractions

A fraction whose top number is smaller than its bottom number is called a proper fraction.

$$\frac{1}{3}$$

1 is smaller than 3.

$$\frac{5}{6}$$

5 is smaller than 6.

$$\frac{2}{7}$$

2 is smaller than 7.

$$\frac{9}{10}$$

9 is smaller than 10.

All proper fractions have a value less than one.

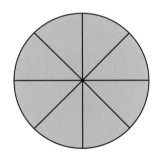

This circle has 8 equal parts. It is one whole circle.

If you are looking at less than 8 parts of the circle, you are looking at less than one whole circle.

$\frac{1}{8}, \frac{2}{8}, \frac{3}{8}, \frac{4}{8}, \frac{5}{8}, \frac{6}{8},$ and $\frac{7}{8}$ are all less than 1.

$\frac{8}{8}$ is the same as 1, so it is not a proper fraction.

Proper fractions can be shown on a number line between the numbers 0 and 1.

Show $\frac{2}{5}$ on a number line.

proper fraction–
A fraction whose top number is smaller than its bottom number.

$\frac{2}{5}$ is less than 1. Draw a number line from 0 to 1.

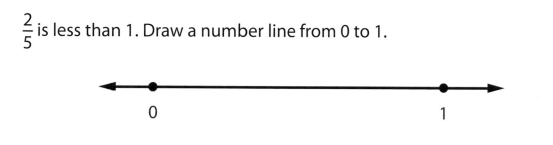

The bottom number (denominator) is 5. That means there are 5 equal parts in one whole. Divide the number line from 0 to 1 into 5 equal spaces.

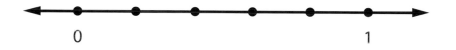

The top number (numerator) is 2. It tells you how many of the sections of the number line you are talking about. The numerator is 2, so count 2 spaces from the 0.

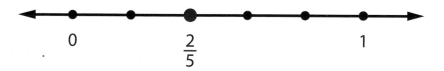

Improper Fractions

An improper fraction has a top number that is equal to or larger than the bottom number.

$$\frac{9}{9}$$

9 is
equal

to 9.

$$\frac{4}{3}$$

4 is
larger

than 3.

$$\frac{7}{6}$$

7 is
larger

than 6.

$$\frac{12}{5}$$

12 is
larger

than 5.

Fractions whose top and bottom number are the same have a value of 1.

A garden is divided into 3 parts. All 3 parts are planted with sunflowers. How much of the garden is planted with sunflowers?

$\frac{3}{3}$ is the same as 1 whole.

The whole garden is planted with sunflowers.

When the top number is larger than the bottom number, the fraction has a value greater than 1.

Here are three halves of a sweater. Three halves is written as the fraction $\frac{3}{2}$.

3 is greater than 2. $\frac{3}{2}$ is greater than 1.

There is more than one sweater.

Mixed Numbers

A mixed number is a mix of two kinds of numbers. There is a whole number, such as 2, and a proper fraction, such as $\frac{1}{4}$.

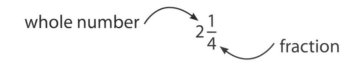

whole number $\quad 2\frac{1}{4} \quad$ fraction

When you read a mixed number out loud, you say the whole number, the word *and*, then the fraction. The mixed number $2\frac{1}{4}$ is read as two and one fourth.

What does a mixed number stand for?

The mixed number $2\frac{1}{4}$ is greater than 2 but less than 3.

 Draw 0 through 3 on a number line.

 Make four equal spaces between the whole numbers 2 and 3.

 The first line you made after the number 2 is $\frac{1}{4}$ more than 2, or $2\frac{1}{4}$.

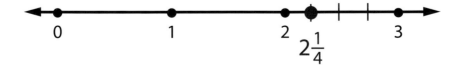

$$0 \qquad 1 \qquad 2 \quad 2\frac{1}{4} \qquad 3$$

14

One page of a sticker book holds 6 famous monster stickers. Marlon has 12 full pages of stickers, and one page with 5 stickers on it. Write the number of pages of stickers as a mixed number.

Write the number of full pages as the whole number part.

12

There are 6 stickers on a full page. Write 6 as the denominator of the fraction part.

$12\frac{}{6}$

There are 5 stickers on the final page. Write 5 as the numerator of the fraction part.

$12\frac{5}{6}$

Marlon has $12\frac{5}{6}$ pages of famous monster stickers.

Comparing Fractions

You can compare two fractions to see which one is greater. If the two fractions have the same denominator, just compare the numerators.

$$\frac{2}{5} \qquad \frac{3}{5}$$

same denominators (5)

numerator—The top number in a fraction.

The numerator 2 is less than the numerator 3, so the fraction $\frac{2}{5}$ is less than the fraction $\frac{3}{5}$.

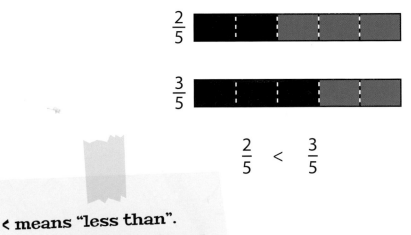

$$\frac{2}{5} \quad < \quad \frac{3}{5}$$

< means "less than".
> means "greater than".

What if the denominators are different? You can easily compare these fractions when the numerators are the same.

$$\frac{1}{3} \qquad \frac{1}{8} \quad \text{— same numerators (1)}$$
$$\qquad\qquad \text{— different denominators}$$

The denominators are different, but the numerators are the same, 1.

$\frac{1}{3}$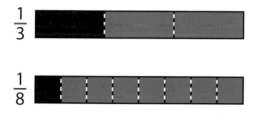

$\frac{1}{8}$

There are the same number of parts in both of these fractions (1 part), but the parts in $\frac{1}{3}$ are larger than the parts in $\frac{1}{8}$.

When the numerators are the same, the fraction with the smaller denominator is the larger fraction.

$$\frac{1}{3} > \frac{1}{8}$$

denominator–The bottom number in a fraction.

Comparing Mixed Numbers

When you are comparing mixed numbers, look at the whole number first.

$$4\frac{2}{3} \qquad 6\frac{1}{2}$$

whole number   whole number

When mixed numbers have different whole number parts (4 and 6), just compare the whole numbers.

4 is less than 6, so $4\frac{2}{3}$ is less than $6\frac{1}{2}$.

$$4\frac{2}{3} \quad < \quad 6\frac{1}{2}$$

mixed number–A number with a whole number and a proper fraction.

e whole number parts, just compare

ɔn

have the same whole

ction parts, $\frac{3}{4}$ and $\frac{1}{4}$.

.

Remember, fractions
must have the same
numerators or
denominators to
be easily compared
(see pages 16 and 17).

Equivalent Fractions

Some fractions, such as $\frac{1}{2}$ and $\frac{3}{6}$, use different numbers but have the same value.

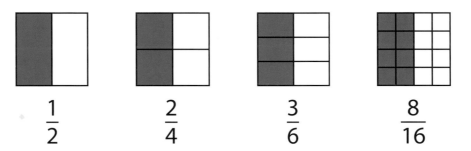

$$\frac{1}{2} \qquad \frac{2}{4} \qquad \frac{3}{6} \qquad \frac{8}{16}$$

All of these fractions ($\frac{1}{2}$, $\frac{2}{4}$, $\frac{3}{6}$, and $\frac{8}{16}$) have equal values. They are called equivalent fractions.

Let's find an equivalent fraction of $\frac{1}{2}$. Multiply or divide the top and bottom number by the same number (other than zero). You can pick any number you like. Let's pick the number 3.

$$\frac{1}{2} \frac{\times 3}{\times 3} = \frac{3}{6}$$

The fractions $\frac{1}{2}$ and $\frac{3}{6}$ are equivalent, or equal.

When there is no number that both the top and bottom number can be divided by, except 1, the fraction is in simplest form.

Put $\frac{4}{12}$ in simplest form.

The numbers 4 and 12 can both be divided by 4.

$$\frac{4}{12} \frac{\div 4}{\div 4} = \frac{1}{3}$$

The fractions $\frac{4}{12}$ and $\frac{1}{3}$ are equivalent. There is no number that both 1 and 3 can be divided by, except 1.

$\frac{4}{12}$ in simplest form is $\frac{1}{3}$.

Estimating Fractions

You can estimate the value of a fraction by comparing the numerator and denominator.

 A When the numerator is about half of the denominator, the value of the fraction is close to $\frac{1}{2}$.

Look at the fraction $\frac{5}{12}$. Half of the denominator, 12, is 6. The numerator, 5, is close to 6, so

$$\frac{5}{12} \text{ is close to } \frac{1}{2}.$$

 B When the numerator is much less than half of the denominator, the value of the fraction is close to 0.

Look at the fraction $\frac{1}{6}$. Half of the denominator, 6, is 3. The numerator, 1, is much less than 3.

$$\frac{1}{6} \text{ is close to } 0.$$

 C When the numerator is much greater than half of the denominator, the value of the fraction is close to 1.

Look at the fraction $\frac{7}{8}$. Half of the denominator, 8, is 4. The numerator, 7, is much greater than 4.

$$\frac{7}{8} \text{ is close to } 1.$$

You can estimate the sum or difference of fractions by estimating the value of each fraction first.

Jamal read $1\frac{3}{8}$ books last week. Then he read another $2\frac{5}{6}$ books this week. About how many books did Jamal read in the two weeks?

First estimate the value of each fraction.

$1\frac{3}{8}$ $\qquad$ $\frac{3}{8}$ is close to $\frac{1}{2}$,

$\qquad\qquad$ so $1\frac{3}{8}$ is close to $1\frac{1}{2}$.

$2\frac{5}{6}$ $\qquad$ $\frac{5}{6}$ is close to 1,

$\qquad\qquad$ so $2\frac{5}{6}$ is close to 3.

Now add the estimated fractions.

$$\begin{array}{r} 1\frac{1}{2} \\ +\, 3 \\ \hline 4\frac{1}{2} \end{array}$$

Jamal read about $4\frac{1}{2}$ books in the two weeks.

Fractions in Measurement

Fractions are used when you measure things. You might measure distance, volume, area, or time. Let's look at measuring distance.

This ruler is 6 inches long. The distance between each numbered line is 1 inch.

Each inch is divided by lines into halves ($\frac{1}{2}$), fourths ($\frac{1}{4}$), and eighths ($\frac{1}{8}$) of an inch.

How long is this grasshopper?

When you measure something with a ruler, line up one end of the object with the zero mark on the ruler.

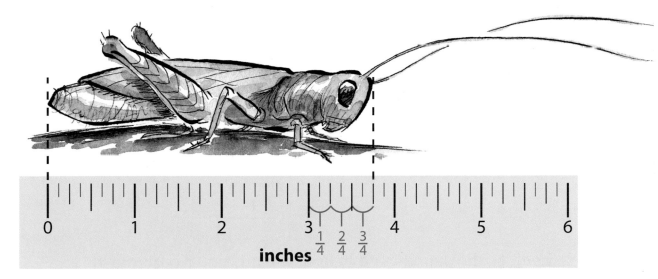

Compare the other end of the object to the ruler. The grasshopper is more than 3 inches long, but not 4 inches long. The end of the grasshopper is at one of the lines that divides an inch into fourths. Count how many fourths longer the grasshopper is than 3 inches.

The grasshopper is $3\frac{3}{4}$ inches long.

Adding Fractions

When you add fractions, first check the denominators. Fractions that have the same denominator are called like fractions.

What is $\dfrac{2}{5} + \dfrac{1}{5}$?

If the fractions have the same denominators, add the numerators and keep the same denominator.

$$\frac{2}{5} + \frac{1}{5} = \frac{2+1}{5} = \frac{3}{5}$$

Remember, the denominator tells how many equal parts are in the whole.

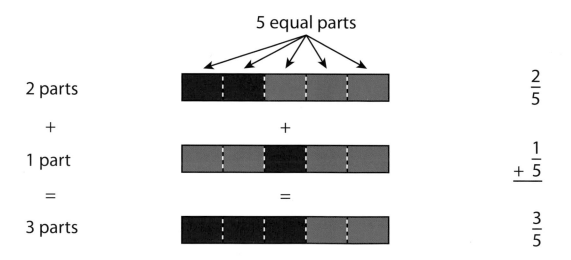

5 equal parts

2 parts		$\dfrac{2}{5}$
+	+	
1 part		$+\dfrac{1}{5}$
=	=	
3 parts		$\dfrac{3}{5}$

Harold made two kinds of soup. The vegetable soup needed $\frac{5}{8}$ cup of onions. The chicken soup needed $\frac{1}{8}$ cup of onions. All together, how many cups of onions did Harold use?

The fractions have the same denominator, so just add the numerators.

$$\frac{5}{8} + \frac{1}{8} = \frac{5+1}{8} = \frac{6}{8}$$

Always put your answers in simplest form. You can divide 6 and 8 by 2.

$$\frac{6 \div 2}{8 \div 2} = \frac{3}{4}$$

Harold used $\frac{3}{4}$ cup of onion for both soups.

Subtracting Fractions

Subtracting fractions works like adding fractions.
Make sure the fractions have the same denominator.

$$\frac{5}{8} - \frac{3}{8}$$

The fractions $\frac{5}{8}$ and $\frac{3}{8}$ are like fractions.
Subtract the top numbers and keep the
bottom number the same.

$$\frac{5}{8} - \frac{3}{8} = \frac{5 - 3}{8} = \frac{2}{8}$$

Always put your answer in simplest form.

$$\frac{2}{8} = \frac{2 \div 2}{8 \div 2} = \frac{1}{4}$$

$$\frac{5}{8} - \frac{3}{8} = \frac{1}{4}$$

A pizza is cut into 6 slices. There were 4 slices, or $\frac{4}{6}$, of the pizza left. Then Gary ate 3 more slices, or $\frac{3}{6}$, of the pizza. What fraction of the pizza is left?

The fractions $\frac{4}{6}$ and $\frac{3}{6}$ are like fractions. Subtract the top numbers and keep the bottom number the same.

$$\frac{4}{6} - \frac{3}{6} = \frac{4-3}{6} = \frac{1}{6}$$

$\frac{1}{6}$ of the pizza is left.

What Is a Decimal?

A decimal number is a number that is written using a decimal point. Decimals have a whole number part, a decimal point, and a decimal part.

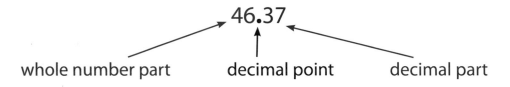

whole number part   decimal point   decimal part

Decimals use place value, just like whole numbers.

tens	ones	decimal point	tenths	hundredths
4	6	.	3	7

In the number 46.37, the digit **3** has a value of 3 tenths, or 0.3.

The digit 7 has a value of 7 hundredths, or 0.07.

You can read any decimal number in four parts.

$$46.37$$

SAY:

1. Read the whole number part.

forty-six

2. Read the decimal point as the word *and*.

and

3. Read the decimal part as if it were a whole number.

thirty-seven

4. Say the place value of the last digit.

hundredths

forty-six and thirty-seven hundredths

Can you read my 54.32 mph FASTBALL??

Decimals and Fractions

A decimal is just another way to write a fraction.

The decimal 0.7 is seven tenths.

The fraction $\frac{7}{10}$ is seven tenths.

$$0.7 \text{ is the same as } \frac{7}{10}.$$

They are even said the same way, seven tenths.

The decimal 1.29 is 1 and 29 hundredths.

The mixed number $1\frac{29}{100}$ is 1 and 29 hundredths.

$$1.29 \text{ is the same as } 1\frac{29}{100}.$$

They are both said the same way, one and twenty-nine hundredths.

Write $\frac{9}{10}$ as a decimal.

1. Write the decimal point. There is no whole number part. Write a zero in the whole number part as a place holder.

   0.

2. Look at the denominator. It is 10, so the last number must be in the tenths place.

   0. __
   ↑

3. Write the numerator so that it ends in the tenths place.

   0.<u>9</u>

Write 8.3 as a mixed number.

1. Write the whole number part.

   8

2. Write the decimal part as the numerator.

   $8\frac{3}{}$

3. Write the place value of the last digit as the denominator.
   The place value is tenths, so write 10.

   $8\frac{3}{10}$

Equivalent Decimals

Some decimals, such as 0.1 and 0.10, have the same value.

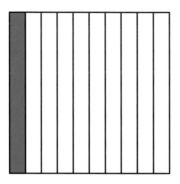

0.1 (one tenth)
of this square is blue

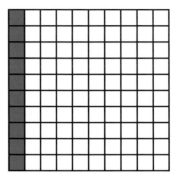

0.10 (ten hundredths)
of this square is blue

These decimals, 0.1 and 0.10, are equal. Decimals that are equal are called equivalent.

Look at the equivalent decimals 0.1 and 0.10.

0.1
0.10

The only difference is the zero on the right. You can add zeros to the right of a decimal number without changing its value.

It does not matter how many zeros you add to the end of a decimal. The value does not change.

$$1.3 =$$
$$1.30 =$$
$$1.300$$

Comparing Decimals

An easy way to compare decimal numbers is to line up the numbers by their place values.

Compare 3.42 and 3.47.

3.42	Write the numbers in a column.
3.47	Line up the decimal points.

Start at the left and compare numbers with the same place values.

3.42	The numbers in the ones place are the same.
3.47	

3.42	The numbers in the tenths place are the same.
3.47	

3.42	The numbers in the hundredths place are different.
3.47	

2 hundredths < 7 hundredths

$$3.42 < 3.47$$

Let's look at another one.

Compare 1.3 and 1.13

1.3	Write the numbers in a column,
1.13	lining up the decimal points.

1.30	You can add a zero to the end of a
1.13	decimal without changing the value
	(see pages 34 and 35).

Start at the left and compare numbers with the same place values.

1.30	The numbers in the ones place
1.13	are the same.

1.30	The numbers in the tenths place
1.13	are different.

3 tenths > 1 tenth

1.3 > 1.13

Rounding Decimals

You round decimal numbers just as you round whole numbers.

The bee hummingbird is the smallest bird in the world. It weighs 0.056 ounces. Round 0.056 to the nearest tenth.

Find the tenths place.   0.0<u>0</u>56

Look at the digit one place to its right.   0.05<u>5</u>6
↑

If the digit is 5 or greater, round up. If the digit is less than 5, round down. The digit is 5, so round the zero in the tenths place up to 1.

0.056 to the nearest tenth is 0.1

38

Rounding is like riding a roller coaster. Let's look at an example.

Round the decimal 2.3 to the nearest whole number.

The whole numbers 2 and 3 are at the bottom of either side of the hill. Evenly spaced between 2 and 3 are the tenths.

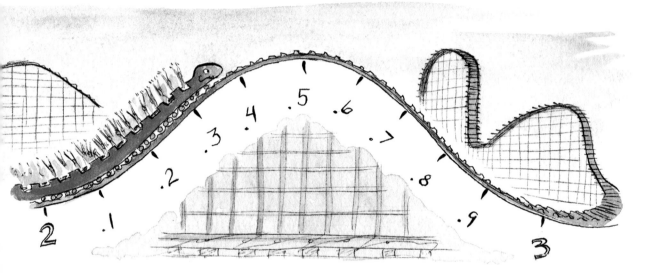

If the roller coaster stops before the top of the hill, 2.5, it will roll back. If the roller coaster stops at 2.5 or more, it will roll forward.

The coaster stopped at 2.3! It will roll back down to the whole number 2.

2.3 to the nearest whole number is 2.

Estimating Decimals

You can use rounding to estimate the answer to an addition or subtraction problem that has decimals.

estimate—To find an answer that is not exact; to make a reasonable guess.

Estimate 12.65 + 2.3.

Round each decimal number to the nearest whole number.	12.65 rounds up to 13 2.3 rounds down to 2
Add the rounded numbers.	13 + 2 = 15

12.65 + 2.3 is about 15.

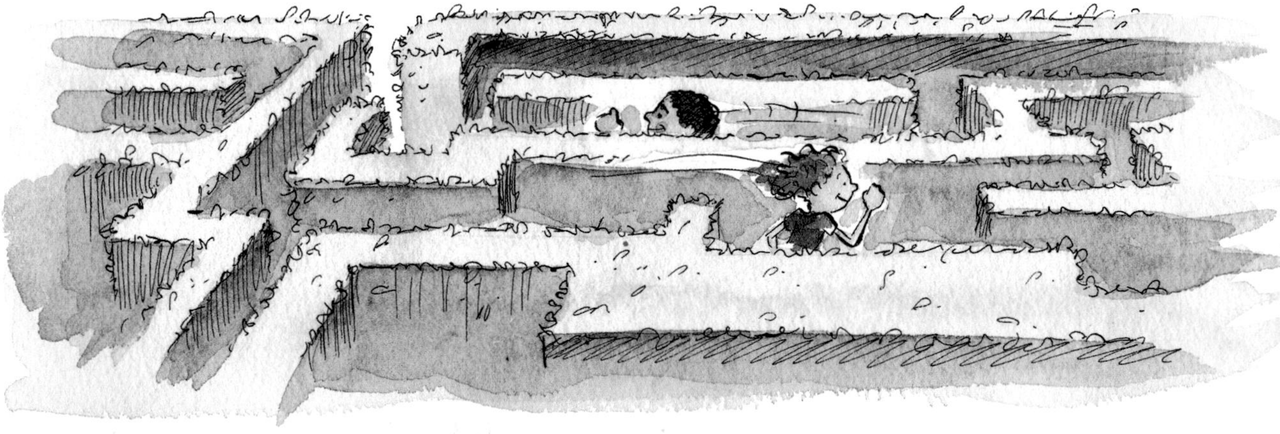

Paco and Jin each finished a maze as quickly as they could. Paco finished in 16.18 seconds. Jin finished in 14.91 seconds. About how much faster did Jin finish the maze than Paco?

You are finding the difference between Paco's time and Jin's time. This is a subtraction problem.

Since the problem asks *about* how much faster, you do not need an exact answer. You can estimate.

Round each decimal number to the nearest whole number.

16.18 rounds down to 16
14.91 rounds up to 15

Subtract the rounded numbers.

$$16 - 15 = 1$$

Jin finished the maze about 1 second faster than Paco.

Adding Decimals

Decimals are added just like whole numbers. An important part of adding decimals is to line up the place values.

$$3.5 + 2.1$$

Write the problem in a column. Use the decimal point to line up place values. Put the decimal point in the answer.

$$\begin{array}{r} 3.5 \\ +\ 2.1 \\ \hline . \end{array}$$

Add right to left, one column at a time.

Add tenths.
$5 + 1 = 6$

$$\begin{array}{r} 3.5 \\ +\ 2.1 \\ \hline .6 \end{array}$$

Add ones.
$3 + 2 = 5$

$$\begin{array}{r} 3.5 \\ +\ 2.1 \\ \hline 5.6 \end{array}$$

$$3.5 + 2.1 = 5.6$$

Money values are written as decimals. Add money the same way you would add any other decimal.

Abby spent $2.37 on an ice cream cone. She also bought a candy bar for $0.59. How much did Abby spend on both?

Add $2.37 and $0.59.

$$
\begin{array}{r}
2.37 \\
+\ 0.59 \\
\hline
.
\end{array}
\qquad
\begin{array}{r}
1 \\
2.37 \\
+\ 0.59 \\
\hline
.\ 6
\end{array}
\qquad
\begin{array}{r}
1 \\
2.37 \\
+\ 0.59 \\
\hline
.96
\end{array}
\qquad
\begin{array}{r}
1 \\
2.37 \\
+\ 0.59 \\
\hline
2.96
\end{array}
$$

Abby spent $2.96 on the ice cream cone and candy bar.

Subtracting Decimals

Decimals are subtracted like whole numbers.

$$5.8 - 4$$

Write the problem in a column.
4 is a whole number, so the
decimal point is after the 4.
Put the decimal point in the answer.

$$\begin{array}{r} 5.8 \\ -\ 4. \\ \hline . \end{array}$$

Write a zero as a place holder in
the tenths place (see pages 34–35).

$$\begin{array}{r} 5.8 \\ -\ 4.0 \\ \hline . \end{array}$$

Subtract right to left, one column at a time.

$$\begin{array}{r} 5.8 \\ -\ 4.0 \\ \hline .8 \end{array} \qquad \begin{array}{r} 5.8 \\ -\ 4.0 \\ \hline 1.8 \end{array}$$

Subtract tenths.   Subtract ones.

$8 - 0 = 8$ $5 - 4 = 1$

$$5.8 - 4 = 1.8$$

Karen rode her bicycle 5.65 miles. John rode 3.16 miles. How much farther did Karen ride?

Subtract to find the difference between Karen's distance (5.65 miles) and John's distance (3.16 miles).

$$\begin{array}{r} {}^{5\ 15} \\ 5.\cancel{6}\cancel{5} \\ -\ 3.16 \\ \hline .\ 9 \end{array}$$

Subtract
hundredths.
$15 - 6 = 9$

$$\begin{array}{r} {}^{5\ 15} \\ 5.\cancel{6}\cancel{5} \\ -\ 3.16 \\ \hline .49 \end{array}$$

Subtract tenths.
$5 - 1 = 4$

$$\begin{array}{r} {}^{5\ 15} \\ 5.\cancel{6}\cancel{5} \\ -\ 3.16 \\ \hline 2.49 \end{array}$$

Subtract ones
$5 - 3 = 2.$

Karen rode her bicycle 2.49 miles farther than John did.

Further Reading

Books

Basher, Simon, and Dan Green. *Math: A Book You Can Count On*. New York: Kingfisher, 2010.

Cleary, Brian P. *A Fraction's Goal—Part of a Whole*. Minneapolis, Minn.: Millbrook Press, 2012.

Franco, Betsy. *Funny Fairy Tale Math*. New York: Scholastic, Inc. 2011.

Mahaney, Ian. F. *Math at the Bank: Place Value and Properties of Operations*. New York: PowerKids Press, 2013.

Internet Addresses

Banfill, J. *AAA Math*. "Fractions." © 2000–2012.
   <http://www.aaamath.com/fra.html>

Math.com. "Homework Help Hot Subject: Decimals." © 2000–2005.
   <http://www.math.com/homeworkhelp/
   HotSubjects_decimals.html>

Math.com. "Homework Help Hot Subject: Fractions." © 2000–2005.
   <http://www.math.com/homeworkhelp/
   HotSubjects_fractions.html>

Index